Written by
SHONDEEN
RAMONTAL-MALCOLM

I AM HUMAN TOO

Illustrated by
JULIA
CHEREDNICHENKO

Archway Publishing books may be ordered through booksellers or by contacting:

Archway Publishing
1663 Liberty Drive
Bloomington, IN 47403
www.archwaypublishing.com
844-669-3957

Because of the dynamic nature of the Internet, any web addresses or links contained in this book may have changed since publication and may no longer be valid. The views expressed in this work are solely those of the author and do not necessarily reflect the views of the publisher, and the publisher hereby disclaims any responsibility for them.

Any people depicted in stock imagery provided by Getty Images are models, and such images are being used for illustrative purposes only. Certain stock imagery © Getty Images.

Interior Image Credit: Julia Cherednichenko

ISBN: 978-1-6657-4306-8 (sc)
ISBN: 978-1-6657-4305-1 (hc)
ISBN: 978-1-6657-4304-4 (e)

Library of Congress Control Number: 2023907955

Print information available on the last page.

Archway Publishing rev. date: 06/27/2023

I am Human Too

This book is dedicated to my brother Timothy "Papi" Ramontal and my beautiful daughters Alessandra and A'Maura Malcolm.

Special Thanks

I am Human too because of my wonderful parents, siblings and loving husband Elvis Malcolm.

First Edition

Shondeen Ramontal-Malcolm, author
Title: I am Human too; Julia Cherednichenko, illustrator
Description: First edition. | Summary: Expressive, Powerful, Advocating is the overarching theme of "I Am Human Too", a children's book for all readers. A celebration of diversity and an imaginative journey to inclusivity. I Am Human Too promotes equity and enables all children to see themselves as equal.
Issued in print format.

Design and handlettering by Julia Cherednichenko
The illustrations for this book were rendered digitally.
Published in the United States of America

SHONDEEN RAMONTAL-MALCOLM

I AM
HUMAN
TOO

Illustrated by
JULIA CHEREDNICHENKO

GRAND THEATER

I am human too!

I may be from across the world.
I may speak a different language.
I may have an accent that you have not
heard before.

I am *human* too.

Selam
Thailand
Вітання з України
嗨
I am from India
ողջույն
Hallo
Warm wishes from
Africa
¡Hola
MUSIC of the WORLD

I may have a darker complexion.
I may have lighter skin.
I may have freckles or birthmarks.

I am *human* too.

I may have straight hair,
I may have kinky hair,
I may have thick hair,
I may have thin hair,
I may have long hair,
I may have short hair,
I may even have no hair.

I am *human* too.

I may be thinner.
I may be chubbier.

I may eat different foods than
you have eaten.
I may cook dishes unfamiliar to you.
I may eat food in a different way.

I am *human* too.

I may walk easily and on my own.
I may need help when I move.
I may move quickly.
I may move slowly.

I am *human* too.

I may speak to friends and family
and new people that I just met.
I may only speak to those closest to me.
I may not be able to speak at all.

I am *human* too.

I may have eyes that work perfectly.
I may need glasses, or see the world
through blurry lenses.
I may not be able to see at all.

I am *human* too.

I may be able to hear everything around me.
I may not know the sounds of the world.
I may hear by feeling vibrations
or reading lips.

I am *human* too.

I may dress differently
than you think I should.
I may shop at different stores or buy
different clothing.
I may make my own clothing.

I am *human* too.

I may be of a different faith.
I may be from a different culture.
I may be spiritual in a different way
than you.
I may not be spiritual at all.

I am *human* too.

I may live in a struggling neighborhood.
I may live in a fancy neighborhood.
I may live in a small house.
I may live in a large house.

I am *human* too.

I may have parents
who both have jobs.

I may have parents
who do not have jobs at all.

I am *human* too.

I may have a mommy and a daddy.
I may have just a mommy
                   or just a daddy.

I may have grandparents or foster parents.
I may be adopted.

I am *human* too.

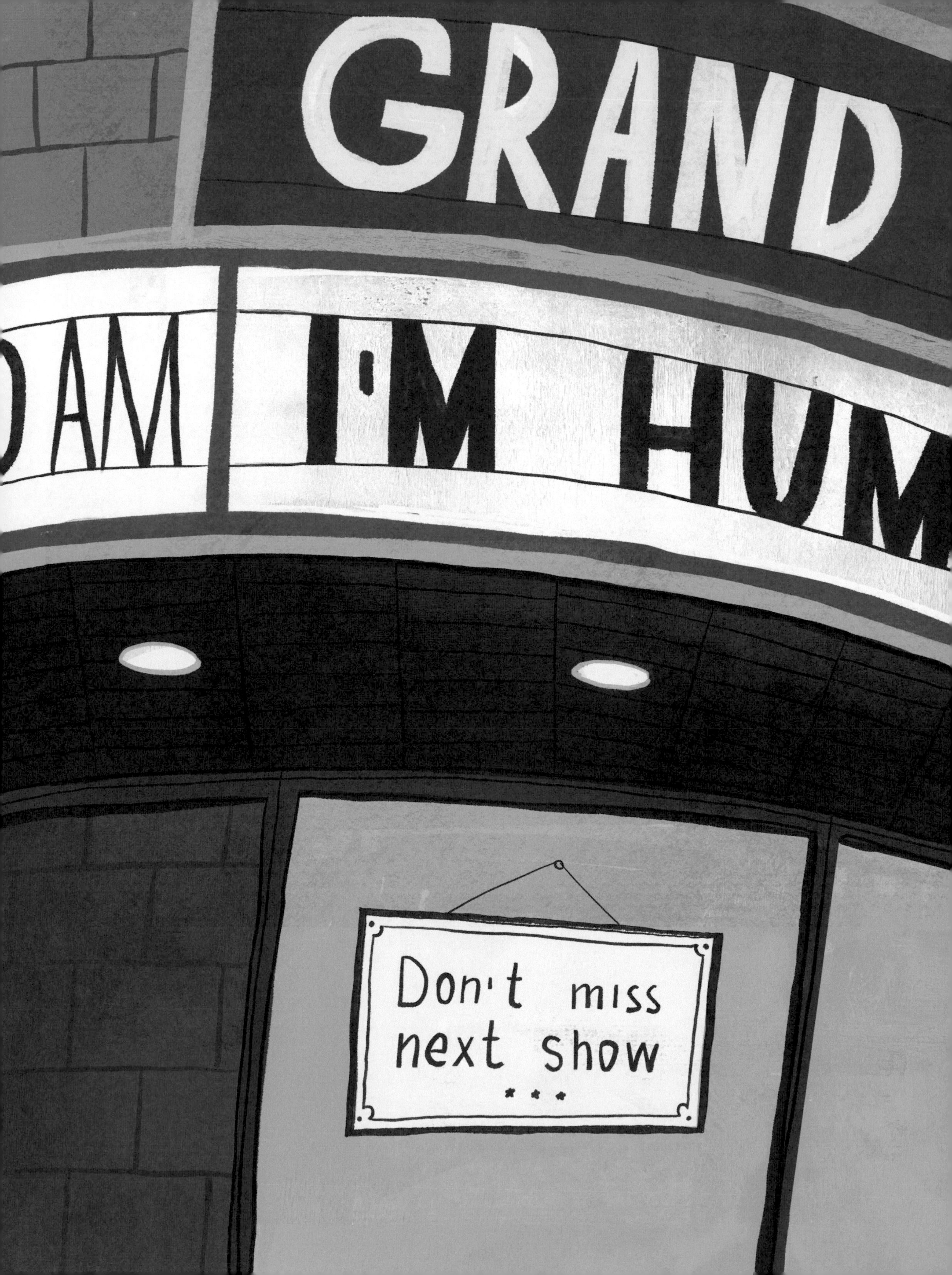
GRAND
DAM
I'M HUM
Don't miss next show
...

I am unique in the life that I live.
You are unique in the life that you live.

We are *all human.*

I am *human* too!

We are unique!
WE ARE ALL
HUMAN
Be KIND to each other ♥

be yourself ..
be kind to yourself

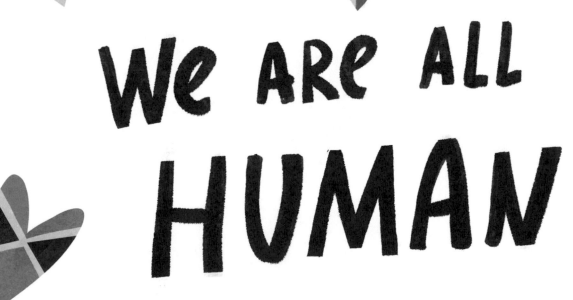

We YOU are
are unique!

WE ARE ALL

HUMAN

Be KIND to each
other ♥

Printed in the United States
by Baker & Taylor Publisher Services